Skyshades

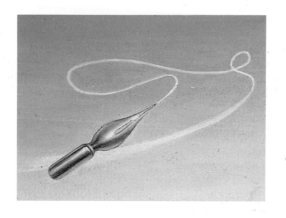

Skyshades

SIXTY SMALL PAINTINGS

BY FANNY BRENNAN

FOREWORD BY CALVIN TOMKINS

A PANACHE PRESS BOOK

CLARKSON POTTER/PUBLISHERS

NEW YORK

Published in the United States by
Clarkson N. Potter, Inc.,
201 East 50th Street, New York, New York 10022

Manufactured in Japan

Library of Congress Cataloging-in-Publication Data
Brennan, Fanny.
Skyshades : sixty small paintings / by Fanny Brennan.—1st ed.
p.   cm.—(A Panache Press Book)
1. Brennan, Fanny—Catalogs. I. Title. II. Series.

ND237.B835A4   1989   89-49557
759.13—DC20   CIP

ISBN 0-517-57671-6
10   9   8   7   6   5   4   3   2   1
First Edition

For my husband, Francis,
and my sons, Christopher and Richard,
with love

FANNY BRENNAN

Who can resist the lure of the small? In childhood we build and people tiny worlds over which we can preside as benevolent giants, invoking the mysterious power of adults. Grown up, and now believing ourselves undeceived, we retain secret selves that submit eagerly, joyfully to the seduction of small, perfect things—netsuke, hummingbirds, pebbles shaped and polished by the sea.

The paintings of Fanny Brennan carry this kind of enchantment. They measure six square inches at their largest (some are barely bigger than postage stamps), and the perfection of their making is such that each one is a miniature world, convincing in all its details. Convincing but unsettling. The imagination that gave rise to them is touched by surrealism, and in particular by Magritte; it is a world where clouds escape from sacks on an empty beach and landscapes peel away at the corner to show different landscapes underneath; where gravity takes time off and the normal scale of things is askew. No sentimentality here, but a darting wit and a mind's eye with a 20/20 fix on paradox.

An American who grew up in Paris between the wars, Fanny Brennan (née Myers) learned classical drawing technique during a brief stint at the Atelier Art et Jeunesse on the Boulevard Saint-Germain, where she always had difficulty filling up the whole space of the large-format drawing paper. (It was more fun hanging out at the Café de Flore nearby; one evening she taught Picasso to play Chinese checkers, while Dora Maar looked on.) Repatriated in 1939, she went to work for *Harper's Bazaar* and then for the Metropolitan Museum of Art. She painted at night in the manner she had arrived at on her own—painted minuscule portraits and landscapes in oil on cut-down pieces of gessoed composition board. Betty Parsons put them into two group shows at the Wakefield Bookshop, which predated the Parsons Gallery. But then, almost before she had begun, Fanny Myers stopped painting. An overseas job with the Office of

War Information took her to London for two years, then to Paris after the liberation. She married Francis Brennan, her boss at O.W.I., and they had two sons, seven years apart. Life took precedence, preempting the intense concentration that this sort of special talent requires.

It was Betty Parsons who got her going again in the 1970s. She took up where she had left off and began showing at the Parsons Gallery and elsewhere. Since then, Fanny Brennan has completed more than three hundred miniature paintings; all together, they would fit neatly inside a medium-size Julian Schnabel. Each one takes her a month or more to do, once she gets the idea for it, and she says she hasn't the foggiest notion where her ideas come from. The ideas her friends and admirers come up with never seem to work. Basically, she paints things she likes—sky, seashells, ribbons, rooms, waterfalls, boxes, lakes, mountains, seacoasts, books, pencils, pen nibs, and small household objects. In the process they become exactly what they are, and a good deal more besides.

Small as they may be, these are real paintings. The touch is sure, and the color, which is both subtle and intense, breathes in a real pictorial space. If there is trickery here, it is not in the painting but in the mind —hers and yours—and more often than not it slips over into pure magic.

CALVIN TOMKINS

11

Reproductions in this book are the exact size

of the artist's original paintings.

BEACH SEWN TO SKY

BASTED WAVES

PACKAGE

COASTAL ROAD

S P O O L S

NIGHT FLIGHT

BALLOON MOON

WALNUT

DOUBLE TREE

TREE SEAT

TAGGED TREE

TREE BOOK

TREE BY STARLIGHT

TREE SKETCH

FOREST

CUTTING CLOUDS

SKY TRIP

PINNING CLOUDS

SACK OF CLOUDS

SKY BUTTON

CLOUD STACKS

SKY SWING

SUMMER READING

FALLING BOOKS

PYRAMIDS

DOMINO BOOKS

FLOATING BOOKS

BOOKS AND ORANGES

BROWN BOOK

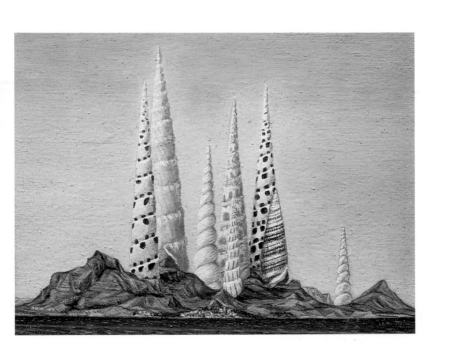

SHELL CITY

IRISH LANDSCAPE

RIBBON SHELL

CLOSE-UP

MAGNET

DOUBLE TIME

PINK HOUSE

MEASURED BUBBLE

CALIPER / CALIPER

SENTRIES

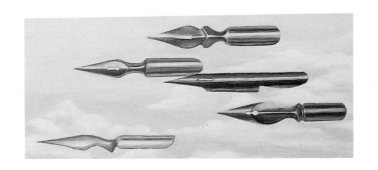

FLYING NIBS

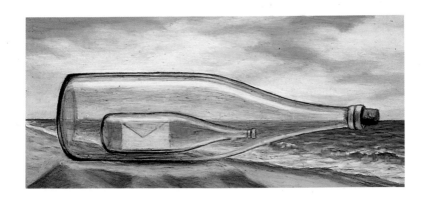

SEA MAIL

PIERCED PEAK

FUNNEL

TROWEL

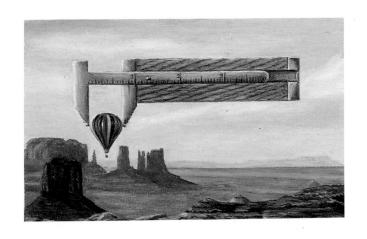

CAPTIVE BALLOON

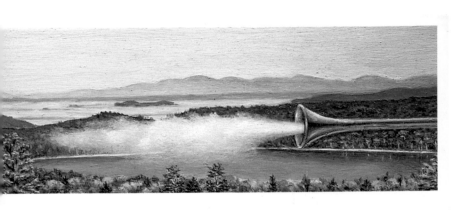

CLARION

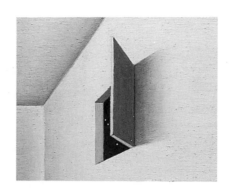

OPEN WINDOW

NIGHT WINDOW

DAY ROOM

NIGHT ROOM

DAY/NIGHT ROOM

CASCADE

BUBBLE

PEARL

FLYAWAY ROAD

REFLECTION

A Q U E D U C T

MONT-SAINT-MICHEL

ART FORMS

FANNY BRENNAN, an American born in Paris and brought up in France, began to paint during her student days. Her work was first shown publicly when she came to New York at the onset of the Second World War. After a hiatus from brushes and canvas of more than twenty years—during which she married, raised a family, and lived in London, Paris, and the United States—she returned to painting. Since then, along with a spate of group exhibitions, she has had six one-woman shows. Mrs. Brennan lives with her husband in New York City.

CALVIN TOMKINS is a definitive chronicler and critic of the art world. His profiles in *The New Yorker* and his published collections of pieces dealing with individual artists and movements from the avant-garde to the neomodern have delighted and enlightened readers over the years. A revised and updated edition of his *Merchants and Masterpieces: The Story of the Metropolitan Museum of Art* appeared last fall. Currently, he is at work on a biography of Marcel Duchamp. Mr. Tomkins lives and works in New York City.

COLLECTORS

Mr. & Mrs. Warren Adelson/*pages 42, 48*
Lily Auchincloss/*pages 26, 62*
Naomi Barry/*page 23*
Ellin Birnham & John Donnelly/*page 35*
Jeffrey & Dana Cooley/*pages 19, 69*
Catherine B. Deely/*page 53*
James & Patricia J. Deely/*page 18*
Louise & Willard Espy/*page 55*
Harmon H. Goldstone/*page 43*
Wilder Green/*page 34*
Philip J. Grove/*page 61*
Robinson A. Grover/*page 50*
Eleanor Lanahan Hazard/*page 30*
Priscilla & Bruce Hubbard/*page 67*
Alice M. Kaplan/*page 49*
Patricia Kind/*page 25*
Mr. & Mrs. R. H. Klein/*pages 63, 71*
Mr. & Mrs. Jack B. Lewus/*page 17*
Mr. & Mrs. Troland S. Link/*page 41*
Mrs. William G. Lord/*page 56*

Book design by Laurence Vétu-Kane
Copywork/transparencies by Michael Burke of Quesada Burke

The artist and the editor are grateful
for the time, trouble, and unstinting
support of the Coe Kerr Gallery.